easy le

Spanish

Ages
5–7

verde

azul

rojo

Me llamo
[My name is]

....

How to use this book

- Look at the left-hand page first to familiarise yourself with the vocabulary being covered.

- Use the pronunciation given for each word to help you to pronounce words correctly. Note that letters in bold are pronounced with more emphasis. There are links to audio files online which will give you further support with pronunciation.

- Read out the instructions clearly and ensure children understand what they have to do.

- Discuss with the children what they have learnt.

- Recap regularly and return to previous topics that the children have enjoyed.

- Reward children with plenty of praise and encouragement.

- Encourage children to say new words out loud. This will help them to practise speaking Spanish, and help them to remember new words.

- Make learning Spanish fun for you and your children!

Special features

- Yellow boxes: introduce and outline the key vocabulary and structures in Spanish.

- Orange boxes: offer suggestions for other activities for children to consolidate their learning in different contexts.

- Orange shaded boxes: provide additional information about Spanish language and culture.

- Blue boxes: give instructions for an activity to reinforce learning.

- Audio symbols ( ): indicate where further activities and support are available online at www.collins.co.uk/homeworkhelp

HarperCollins Publishers
Westerhill Road
Bishopbriggs
Glasgow
G64 2QT

First Edition 2019
10 9 8 7 6 5 4 3 2 1

© HarperCollins Publishers 2019

ISBN 978-0-00-831275-6

www.collins.co.uk

Printed and bound in
Great Britain by Martins the Printers

The contents of this publication are believed correct at the time of printing. Nevertheless the Publisher can accept no responsibility for errors or omissions, changes in the detail given or for any expense or loss thereby caused.

A catalogue record for this book is available from the British Library.

MANAGING EDITOR
Maree Airlie

FOR THE PUBLISHER
Laura Waddell
Sarah Woods

CONTRIBUTORS
Cristina Llompart

ILLUSTRATIONS
Q2AMedia

MAPS
© Collins Bartholomew Ltd

IMAGES
cover: © James Weston/Shutterstock
pg28: © RedlineVector/Shutterstock

MIX
Paper from
responsible sources
FSC™ C007454

FSC
www.fsc.org

This book is produced from independently certified FSC™ paper to ensure responsible forest management.

For more information visit: www.harpercollins.co.uk/green

Contents

El alfabeto en español
The Spanish alphabet

The Spanish alphabet has the same letters as in English, plus one extra letter. Can you spot it?

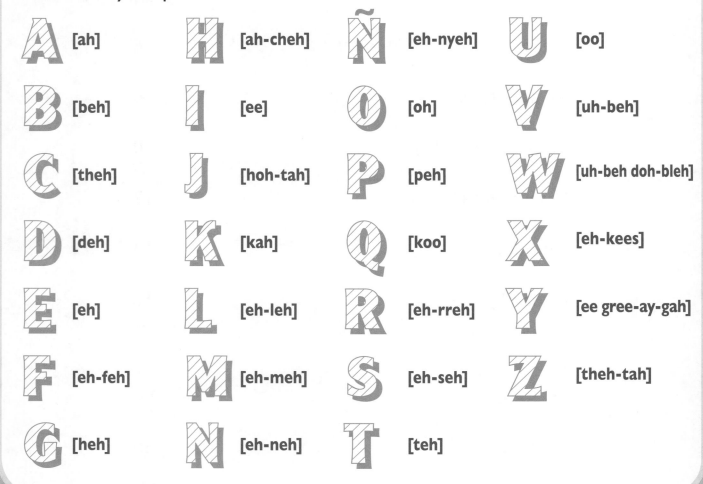

A [ah]

B [beh]

C [theh]

D [deh]

E [eh]

F [eh-feh]

G [heh]

H [ah-cheh]

I [ee]

J [hoh-tah]

K [kah]

L [eh-leh]

M [eh-meh]

N [eh-neh]

Ñ [eh-nyeh]

O [oh]

P [peh]

Q [koo]

R [eh-rreh]

S [eh-seh]

T [teh]

U [oo]

V [uh-beh]

W [uh-beh doh-bleh]

X [eh-kees]

Y [ee gree-ay-gah]

Z [theh-tah]

Try singing the Spanish alphabet to the same tune as the English one or even to "Auld Lang Syne". You could play "Hangman", called **El ahorcado** in Spanish, using children's names or film characters, saying the letters in Spanish.

 Track 1

Did you know? Spanish is not just spoken in Spain. It is also the national language in many other countries, like most of South and Central America, Mexico and Equitorial Guinea in Africa. It is also widely spoken in the United States.

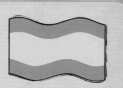

Join the letters of the alphabet in order to draw this famous Spanish landmark. Once you have completed the picture, say the whole alphabet out loud.

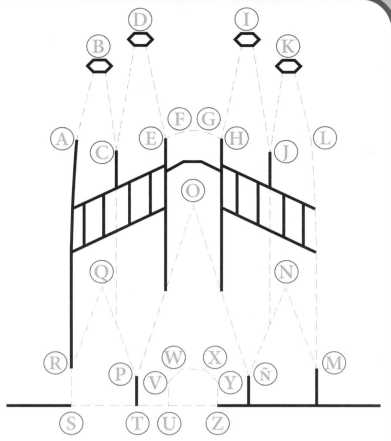

Find out its name by replacing the missing letters using the pronunciation clue underneath:

L _ SA _ RA _ A _ AMIL _ A
ah   heh   deh eh-feh   ee

Write out your name in fancy letters – bubble writing, different colour pens, dot to dot – and practise saying each letter in Spanish as you do it.

¡Hola!
Hello!

When you first start speaking Spanish you want to be able to say the simple things. These two children are using Spanish to greet each other.

¡Hola!
(Hello!)

¿Qué tal?
(How are you?)

Bien, gracias.
(Fine, thanks.)

¡Hola!
(Hi!)

¡Adiós!
(Goodbye!)

¡Adiós!
(Bye!)

These words are pronounced like this:

hola	¿qué tal?	gracias
[**o**lah]	[**keh** tal]	[**gra**theeass]

adiós	bien
[adee**oss**]	[bee-**en**]

Other things you might like to say are:

sí [see] meaning **yes** and **no** [noh] meaning **no**

por favor [por fah**vor**] meaning **please**

de nada [deh **nah**dah] meaning **you're welcome**

así, así [ah**see**, ah**see**] meaning **not too bad**

Use your fingers or make sock puppets to act out a short conversation, practising saying **hola** and **adiós** and asking after each other. Why not give your puppets a name and use them throughout this book to practise speaking Spanish?

Did you know? In Spain, people often kiss each other on both cheeks when they meet.

Look carefully at the Spanish words given below and circle the one that is the odd one out. Can you also pronounce these words in Spanish and say what they mean in English?

no	no	os	no	no
hola	hola	hola	hola	ola
gracias	gracias	grande	gracias	gracias
sí	sí	sí	mí	sí

Use different coloured pencils to go over the dots to write out this Spanish word. What does it say?

Upside down!

When you are writing a question in Spanish there is always an upside-down question mark at the start of the question as well as at the end. The picture shows you how to write one. Start at the top and have a go!

Another sign appears upside down in Spanish as well. Look again at the conversation on page 6 and see if you can spot which one!

Todo sobre mí
All about me

One of the things you will want to do in Spanish is to introduce yourself:
Me llamo... [meh **ya**mo] **My name is...**

If you want to ask someone's name you can say:
¿Cómo te llamas? [**koh**moh teh **yah**mas]
What is your name?

 Track 2

Play this game with a partner: make a list of characters like the ones shown below. Choose a character for your partner to be. That person then has to guess which character you have chosen for them by asking **¿Me llamo...? Is my name...?** If they get it right, say **sí**, if they don't, say **no**, and they can try again. Make sure you both get a turn. Why not think of other characters, for example, cartoon characters, to play this game?

Ziggy   **Bella**   **Nellie**   **Igor**   **Frosty**

Did you know? Lots of names in English have a different form in Spanish, for example, Andrew in Spanish is Andrés, Michael is Miguel and Peter is Pedro. Lots of girls' names in English already come from Spanish, for example, Lola, Carmen and Angela.

Draw a picture of yourself in the picture frame below. On the lines below write **hola** and fill in your name.

¡ _____ !

Me llamo _____ .

Sé contar (1-10)
I can count (1-10)

Here are the numbers you need to count up to ten in Spanish:

1
uno
[**oo**noh]

2
dos
[doss]

3
tres
[trehss]

4
cuatro
[**kwa**tro]

5
cinco
[**think**oh]

6
seis
[sayss]

7
siete
[see-**eh**teh]

8
ocho
[**oh**choh]

9
nueve
[**nwe**veh]

10
diez
[dee-**eth**]

Many numbers end in **o**. Say it like the "o" in "pot". The **c** in **cinco** is like "th" as in "think", but in **cuatro** it is a "c" as in "cat".

Other things you might like to say are:

más [mass] meaning **add**   **menos** [**meh**noss] meaning **take away**

igual [ee**gual**] meaning **equals**

 Track 3

Practise counting in Spanish in different ways – loudly and quietly, singing the numbers, even backwards from ten. Ask a partner to hold out their fingers and close their eyes. Number the fingers from 1 to 10, then touch any finger and ask them to say what number it is in Spanish.

Did you know? Lots of Spanish people write the number 7 with a line across it, like this: ⁊ This is so that it doesn't get confused with the number 1, which can sometimes be written with a little "hat" on it, like this: *1*

Look at these pictures and count the objects in Spanish out loud.
Write the correct number under each picture.

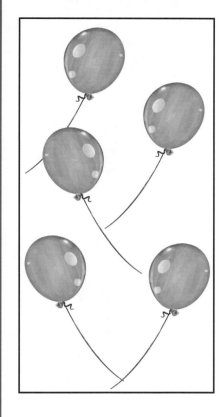

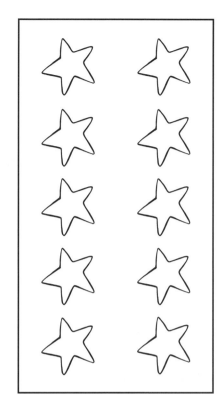

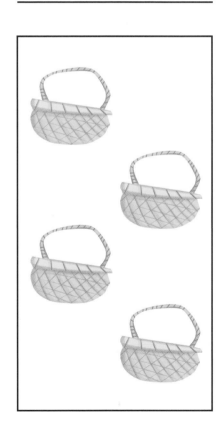

Sé contar (11-20)
I can count (11-20)

Here are the numbers you need to count up to twenty in Spanish:

11
once
[**on**-theh]

12
doce
[**doh**-theh]

13
trece
[**treh**-theh]

14
catorce
[ka**tor**-theh]

15
quince
[**keen**-theh]

16
dieciséis
[**dyeh**thee-**sayss**]

17
diecisiete
[**dyeh**thee-**see-eh**teh]

18
dieciocho
[**dyeh**thee-**oh**choh]

19
diecinueve
[**dyeh**thee-**nwe**veh]

20
veinte
[**bayn**teh]

 Track 4

Work with a partner and count together or alternately up to 20, clapping your hands and knees while you are doing it. Speed up and slow down, trying to keep the same rhythm. Why not try some simple sums, using dice or playing cards?

Did you know? In Spain, mobile numbers start with 6 or 7.

Juego: Bingo

Let's play ¡Bingo! Choose 5 numbers between 1 and 10 or 1 and 20 and write them down. Listen for your numbers to be called out in Spanish – if you have written the number down on the sheet, you can score it off. If you manage to score all the numbers off, shout "¡bingo!"

Juego 1

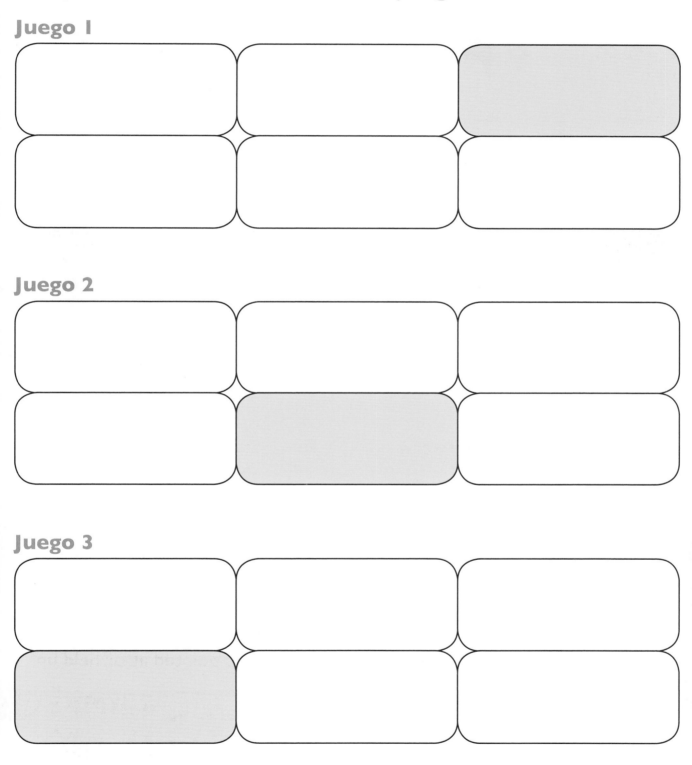

Juego 2

Juego 3

Los colores
Colours

These are the names of some of the colours in Spanish:

azul
[ah**thul**]

rojo
[**ro**ho]

verde
[**bair**deh]

amarillo
[ahmah**ree**yo]

blanco
[**blan**koh]

negro
[**neh**groh]

rosa
[**roh**sah]

violeta
[bee-oh**leh**tah]

naranja
[nah**rahn**ha]

marrón
[mah**rron**]

If you want to ask what colour something is, ask: **¿De qué color es?** [deh keh koh**lohr** ess]. The answer would be: **Es...** [ess] **It is...**

 Track 5

Play a version of "I spy" in Spanish using colours rather than letters:
Veo algo... [**bay**oh **al**goh....] **I can see something...**
Guesses can be given in English or the object can be pointed at or held up.

Did you know? In Spain, the Spanish football team is known as La Roja which means **The red one,** and sometimes as La Furia Roja, which means **Red Fury.**

The Spanish flag is made up of two colours. Can you colour it using the words below? Then try to copy the coat of arms onto the flag.

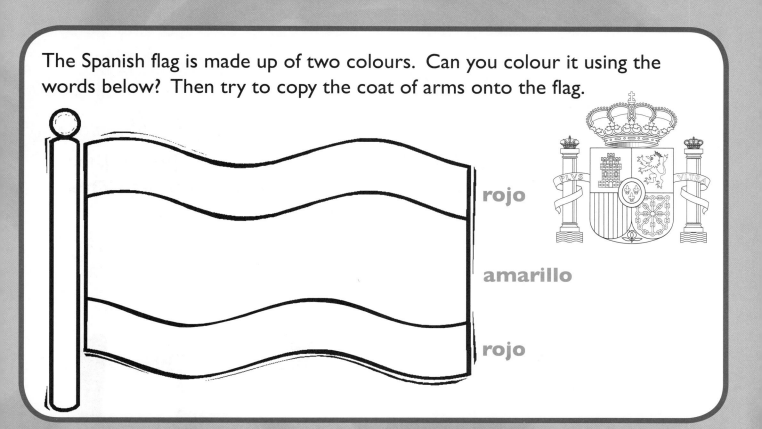

rojo

amarillo

rojo

Colour in the rainbow – **arcoíris** [**ar**koh**ee**rees] – using the colours given in Spanish. There is a key under the picture to help you get the colours right.

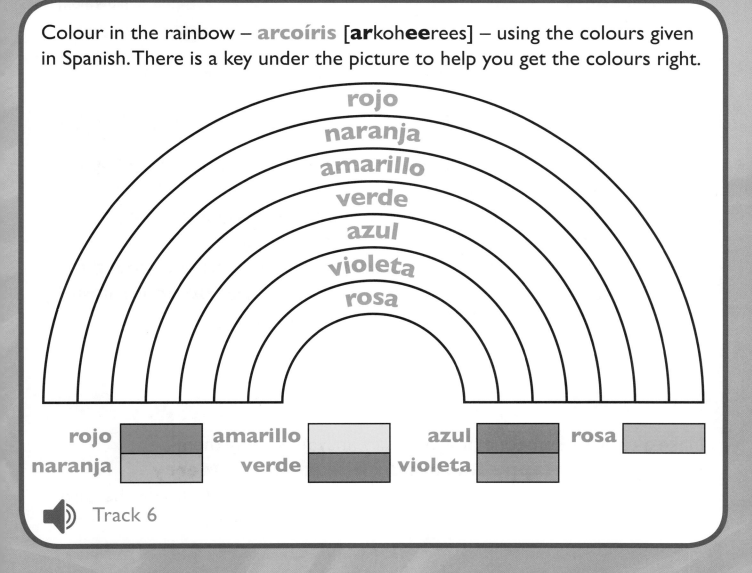

rojo
naranja
amarillo
verde
azul
violeta
rosa

rojo		amarillo		azul		rosa	
naranja		verde		violeta			

Track 6

15

Mi familia
My family

To introduce members of your family, you can say: **Este es...** [**es**te es], for boys or men, and **Esta es** [**es**ta es], for girls or women, which mean **This is...** Remember to use **mi** [mee] to say my...

Esta es mi...   Este es mi...

hermana
[air**mah**nah]

mamá
[mah**mah**]

abuela
[ab**we**lah]

papá
[pah**pah**]

hermano
[air**mah**noh]

abuelo
[ab**we**loh]

To talk about how many brothers or sisters you have, use **Tengo** [**te**ngoh] meaning **I have**, for example: **Tengo una hermana** or **Tengo un hermano**. Remember to use **una** [**oo**nah] for sisters and **un** [oon] for brothers. You can combine the sentences using **y** [ee]: **Tengo dos hermanas y un hermano**. If you want to ask someone else about their family, you can say: **¿Tienes una hermana?** [tee-**en**es **oo**nah air**mah**nah] or **¿Tienes un hermano?** [tee-**en**es oon air**mah**noh].

 Track 7

Make a card for someone in your family, maybe wishing them **feliz cumpleaños** (**Happy Birthday**), **feliz Navidad** (**Merry Christmas**) or **¡Enhorabuena!** (**Congratulations!**). Inside the card you could write **para** meaning **to** and **de** meaning **from**.

Introduce some members of your family using **Este es mi** (for boys and men) or **Esta es mi** (for girls and women). Then write their name after **¡Hola!**

Este es mi _____

¡Hola _____ !

Esta es mi _____

¡Hola _____ !

Esta es mi _____

¡Hola _____ !

Esta es mi _____

¡Hola _____ !

Este es mi _____

¡Hola _____ !

Las mascotas
Pets

Pets can be just as important as other family members. To talk about your pets you can use **Tengo** [**te**ngoh] as you did when talking about your family.

un **perro**
[oon **per**roh]

un **pez**
[oon peth]

un **conejo**
[oon ko**ne**ho]

un **hámster**
[oon **ham**ster]

un **gato**
[oon **gat**oh]

un **conejillo de Indias**
[oon ko**ne**heeyo deh **een**dyas]

un **caballo**
[oon ka**ba**yoh]

una **tortuga**
[**oo**nah tor**too**gah]

If you want to ask whether someone has a pet, you can say: **¿Tienes una mascota** [tee-**en**es **oo**na mas**ko**tah]. The answer could be either **Sí, tengo...** or **No**. Remember to use **un** [oon] or **una** [**oo**nah] for the different pets. You can combine the sentences using **y** [ee]: **Tengo una tortuga y un hámster.**

🔊 Track 8

Work with a partner – one person acts out an animal, the other tries to guess what that animal is in Spanish: **¿Es un/una...?** [ess oon/**oo**nah] **Is it a...?** The answer would then be **sí** or **no**. You could learn a few more exotic animals to make it more fun, for example, **una serpiente** [**oo**nah sehr**pye**nteh] – a **snake**, or even **una tarántula** [**oo**nah ta**ran**toolah] – a **tarantula!** To make your acting more authentic, why not make masks of the animals that you can wear?

Did you know? Dogs in Spanish say **guau, guau** [wow wow], birds sing **pío pío** [pee-o pee-o], and pigs go **oinc, oinc** [oheenk, oheenk]!

Juego: Sopa de letras

Can you find these six Spanish pets in the square?

caballo   pez   gato   perro   conejo   tortuga

h	r	t	o	y	t	c
c	o	n	e	j	o	a
p	e	z	i	u	r	b
e	m	t	n	n	t	a
r	s	x	v	b	u	l
r	g	a	t	o	g	l
o	g	w	i	r	a	o

Why not make up your own **Sopa de letras** using some Spanish words for pets?

_____

_____

_____

_____

_____

Mi cuerpo
My body

If you want to talk about different parts of the body in Spanish, here are the most common words you might need.

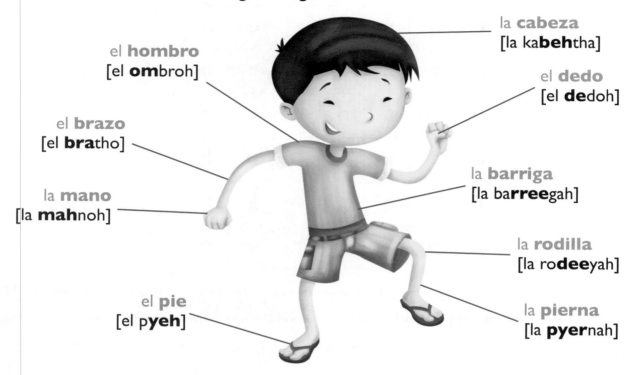

el **hombro**
[el **om**broh]

el **brazo**
[el **bra**tho]

la **mano**
[la **mah**noh]

el **pie**
[el p**yeh**]

la **cabeza**
[la ka**beh**tha]

el **dedo**
[el **de**doh]

la **barriga**
[la ba**rree**gah]

la **rodilla**
[la ro**dee**yah]

la **pierna**
[la **pyer**nah]

In order to practise these words, it might be helpful to learn the instruction **tócate...** [**tok**ahteh] – **touch your...**

 Track 9

Take a large piece of paper and draw the outline of a body on it, or even draw round someone lying on a very large piece of paper. Write the words for different parts of the body on sticky notes, then stick them on to the body in the correct place. You could put them on incorrectly and see if anyone spots which part is wrong!

Did you know? The word for **toe** in Spanish is el dedo del pie [el **de**doh del p**yeh**] which actually means "the finger on the foot".

Juego: Beetle Drive

A good way to practise the words for parts of the body is to play a game of "Beetle Drive". The aim of the game is to draw a full person by rolling the appropriate numbers on the dice – each number represents a part of the body. Use the boxes below to draw in.

You need to roll a 6 first to start the game and draw **el cuerpo**, then add on the other body parts as you roll them on the dice. The first player to complete their person shouts out "**¡Terminado!**" [termee**na**doh] meaning **finished!** **¡Buena suerte!** – **good luck!**

Numbers for each part of the body

1 = la **cabeza**   2 = la **pierna**   3 = el **brazo**   4 = el **pie**

5 = la **mano**   6 = el **cuerpo**

Juego 1

Juego 2

Juego 3

Juego 4

Mi cara
My face

To talk about specific parts of your face in Spanish, use the following vocabulary.

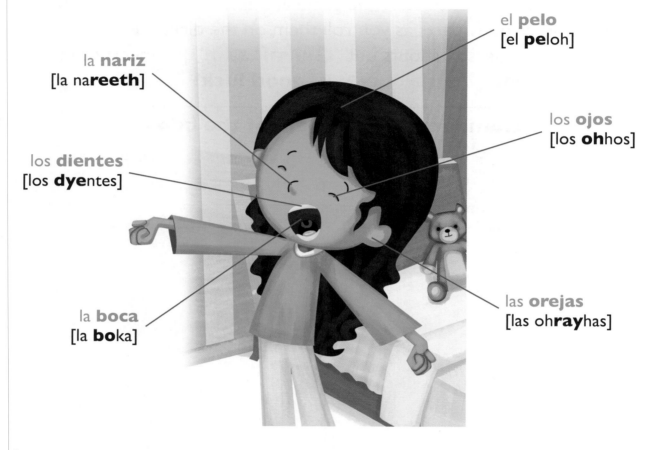

el **pelo**
[el **pe**loh]

la **nariz**
[la na**reeth**]

los **ojos**
[los **oh**hos]

los **dientes**
[los **dye**ntes]

las **orejas**
[las oh**ray**has]

la **boca**
[la **bo**ka]

🔊 Track 10

The Spanish equivalent to the game "Simon says" is called **Simón dice** and is played in the same way. Instructions could be: **tócate...** [**to**kahteh] – **touch your...** or **mueve...** [**moo-eh**beh] – **move...** Of course, it is always fun to sing "Heads, shoulders, knees and toes" in Spanish: **la cabeza, los hombros, las rodillas y los pies... los ojos, las orejas, la boca y la nariz.**

Did you know? If you want to say that someone talks a lot in Spanish, you can use the phrase **hablar por los codos** which actually means **to talk through the elbows**!

Draw a monster's head, using your imagination to make it look as strange as you can! Write down the number of eyes, ears and so on that you have given your monster and show what colours you have used in the box below.

	Número	Color
boca		
ojos		
orejas		
dientes		
nariz		

Mi estuche
My pencil case

Here are the Spanish words for some of the items that might be found in a pencil case.

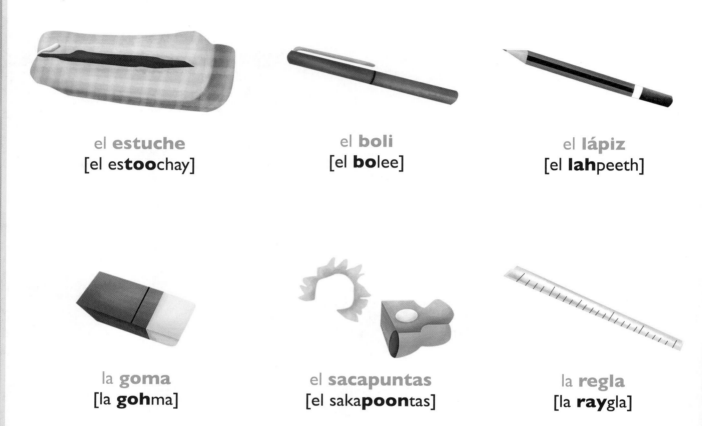

el **estuche**
[el es**too**chay]

el **boli**
[el **bo**lee]

el **lápiz**
[el **lah**peeth]

la **goma**
[la **goh**ma]

el **sacapuntas**
[el saka**poon**tas]

la **regla**
[la **ray**gla]

Playing "Kim's Game" is a great way to practise Spanish vocabulary and can be used with the objects above. Place some of the above items on the table for others to see and remember (in Spanish). When their eyes are closed, remove one object, saying ¿Qué falta? [keh **fal**tah] – **What's missing?** Of course, only answers in Spanish will be accepted. This game can be used to practise colours (using coloured pencils) too.

Did you know? Spanish schools usually start at 9, and most finish at 2 o'clock in the afternoon, which is when people have lunch in Spain. However, some schools carry on until 4 o'clock and have a long break for lunch.

Design your ideal pencil case. Remember to include a space for **el lápiz, la goma, los bolis** and anything else you want to keep in it. You might want to label it in Spanish too.

Draw the correct number of items in each box. Practise counting as you draw.

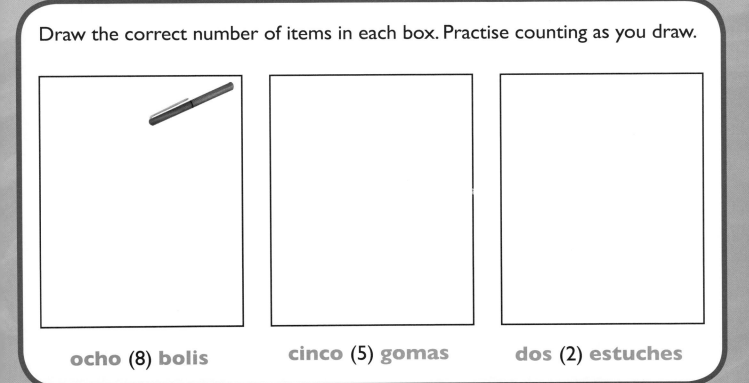

ocho (8) **bolis**   **cinco** (5) **gomas**   **dos** (2) **estuches**

Sé...
I can...

On this page you can show how well you feel you have done while you have been learning Spanish. Fill in the table to show your progress for each topic you have been learning.

 muy bien

 bien

 así, así

Sé hablar de... I can talk about...	
...el alfabeto en español ...the Spanish alphabet	
...mí ...me	
...los números 1-10 ...the numbers 1-10	
...los números 11-20 ...the numbers 11-20	
...los colores ...colours	
...mi familia ...my family	
...los animales ...pets	
...mi cuerpo ...my body	
...mi cara ...my face	
...mi estuche ...my pencil case	

¡**Bravo!** You have learned how to say so many things in Spanish. Colour in the letters and pictures and fill in your name and date to make your very own personalised certificate.

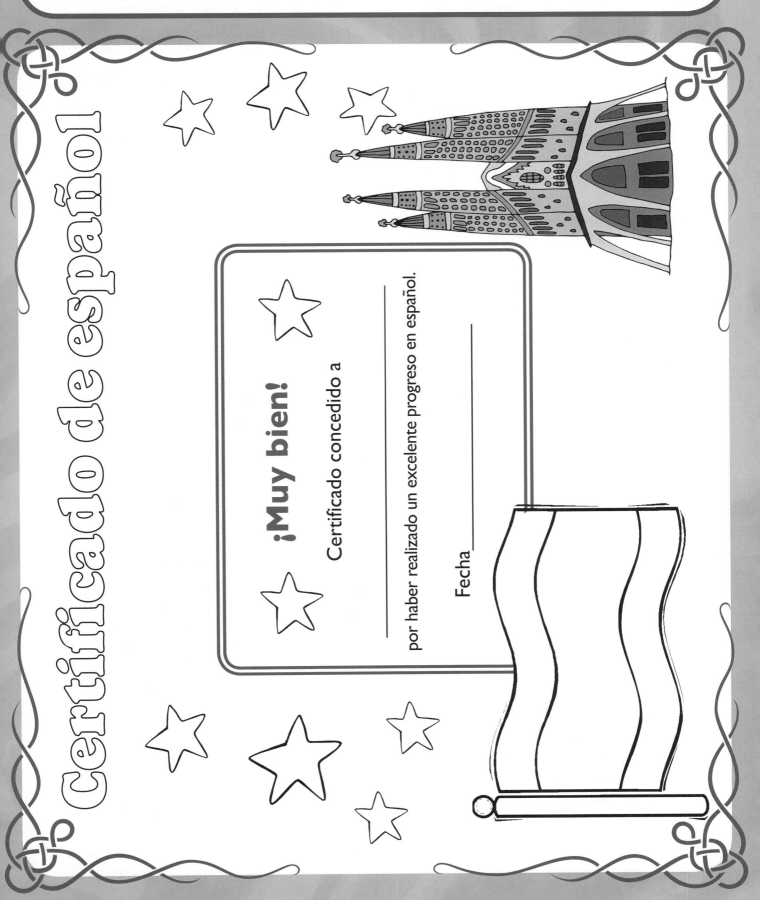

Certificado de español

¡Muy bien!

Certificado concedido a

por haber realizado un excelente progreso en español.

Fecha

El mapa de España
Map of Spain

The map below shows Spain and some of its most important features.

Did you know? There are another four languages spoken in Spain: Basque, Catalan, Galician and Valencian. Spanish, which is the official language for the whole of Spain, is also known there as Castillian.

Did you know? The range of mountains that separates Spain and France is called the Pyrenees. It is a great area for walking and skiing.

SPAIN

Did you know?
La Sagrada Familia in Barcelona is an unfinished cathedral. Its architect, Gaudi, started buiding it over 135 years ago but died before he could finish it. Its construction is still going on!

Did you know? The south of Spain has beautiful Arab palaces and buildings such as the Alhambra in Granada and the Mosque in Cordoba. This is because the Arabs lived in Spain for over 700 years.

Espańa y Europa
Spain and Europe

The map below shows Spain and the countries that are close to Spain.

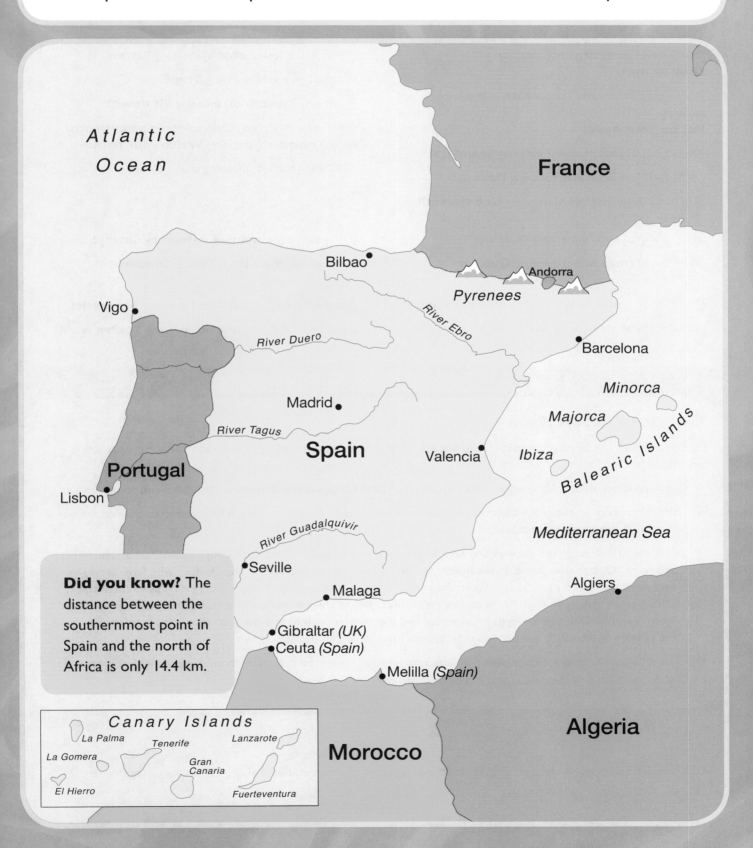

Atlantic Ocean

France

Bilbao

Andorra

Pyrenees

River Ebro

Vigo

River Duero

Barcelona

Minorca

Madrid

Majorca

River Tagus

Spain

Valencia

Ibiza

Balearic Islands

Portugal

Lisbon

Mediterranean Sea

River Guadalquivir

Did you know? The distance between the southernmost point in Spain and the north of Africa is only 14.4 km.

Seville

Malaga

Algiers

Gibraltar *(UK)*

Ceuta *(Spain)*

Melilla *(Spain)*

Canary Islands

La Palma

Tenerife

Lanzarote

La Gomera

Gran Canaria

El Hierro

Fuerteventura

Morocco

Algeria

Additional suggestions for language practice

The next two pages give some suggestions for games and activities that can be used with larger groups of children, for example, in class or at Spanish out-of-school organisations, holiday clubs and so on.

It is often useful to have some basic commands in Spanish and some of these listed below may be helpful. All the instructions are in the plural form to talk to more than one child.

¡Miradme! [mee**rath**meh] meaning **Look at me!**

¡Levantad la mano! [lehban**tath** la **mah**noh] meaning **Put up your hand!**

¡Levantaos! [leban**ta**h-os] meaning **Stand up!**

¡Dibujad! [deeboo**hath**] meaning **Draw...!**

¡Empezad! [empe**thath**] meaning **Get started!**

¡Rápido! [**ra**peedoh] meaning **Quickly!**

¡Más bajo! [**mas ba**ho] meaning **Quieter!**

¡Muy bien! [**moo**-ee bee-**en**] meaning **Very good!**

¡Bravo! [**bra**boh] meaning **Well done!**

¡Escuchad! [eskoo**chath**] meaning **Listen!**

¡Parad! [pa**rath**] meaning **Stop!**

¡Sentáos! [sen**tah**-os] meaning **Sit down!**

¡Escribid vuestro nombre! [eskree**beeth** boo-**es**troh **nom**breh] meaning **Write your name!**

¡Vamos! [**ba**mos] meaning **Go!**

¡Despacio! [des**pah**theeoh] meaning **Slowly!**

¡Más alto! [**mas al**to] meaning **Louder!**

¡Fantástico! [fan**tas**teekoh] meaning **Fantastic!**

¡Has ganado! [as ga**na**doh] meaning **You've won!**

Outdoor activities

Lots of activities can be played outside, including standard children's games but with a Spanish twist. Here are just a few ideas:

- Send children off on a "Scavenger Hunt", looking for una cosa verde/amarilla/marrón and so on.

- Write numbers on the ground with chalk, shout out numbers or sums and children have to run to the correct one – this could also be played in teams.

- Children stand up against the wall and each is given one of 4 Spanish words, for example, colours, pets, numbers and so on. One person stands in the middle and shouts out one of the words. The children who have been given that word try to run past the catcher in the middle without getting caught. Anyone caught helps to catch the others when they are called. Another version of this is where children stand in a circle and are each given one of 4 Spanish words. One of the words is called out and the children who have been given that word have to run round the outside of the circle and back to their space. The last person back sits down.

- Use a parachute to practise colours – children have to run under the parachute to swap places with someone else who is also holding the colour that has been called out.

Did you know? Spanish children sing this hand-clapping song that sometimes is also used as a choosing rhyme:
Choco-choco-la-la, Choco-choco-te-te, Choco-la, Choco-te, ¡Cho-co-la- te!

Active games

There are many ways to incorporate Spanish into games which can be played in an indoor (or outdoor) space. Some examples of these are:

- Play "Corners" – put a picture in each corner of the area. The pictures could be of, for example, **los colores, la familia, los animales**. Children move around the room and on a signal they go to stand in one of the corners. A corner is called out in Spanish by the leader and the children in that corner are out. Keep playing until only a winner is left.

- Stand in a circle with the first child counting either 1 or 1, 2 or 1, 2, 3 in Spanish and the next child continuing from there, saying an additional one, two or three numbers. Keep counting around the circle until someone says 13. That person then sits down and the game begins again, until there is only one person left.

- Ask children to move around the room – **rápido/despacio** – and when they hear a part of the body they have to find a partner and touch those parts of the body together.

- Sit in a circle and give each child one of 4 or 5 Spanish words belonging to a particular category, for example, pets, colours, family members. One child stands in the middle of the circle and calls out one of these words. Each child who has been given that word has to swap places with someone else with that word. The one person left in the middle is the next person to choose the word.

Quiet activities

There are lots of ideas to consolidate learning in Spanish through activities that do not require too much space or moving around. Below are just a few ideas:

- Use building blocks to practise Spanish numbers and colours – one child could describe a tower they have built and see if others can copy it without seeing it.

- "Consequences" is a fun way of reinforcing basic language. Each child has a piece of paper. At the top they have to answer the question **¿Cómo te llamas?** in a sentence, then fold over the paper and pass it to the person beside them. The next person answers the question **¿Tienes una mascota?**, folds over the paper and passes it on. This can continue with questions and answers, with the paper being folded over and passed on each time. Finally, the paper is unfolded and the answers read out – it usually makes for a funny story!

- Call out the alphabet, a letter at a time. If a child hears one of the letters in their name, they need to stand up and say **¡yo!** before sitting down again and waiting for the next letter.

- Dice are great for practising numbers and can also be used in other activities. Draw 6 pets and number them 1-6: ask a child to roll the dice and tell you which animal they have rolled. This could be used for other word categories, or extend the game from 1-12 and use two dice added together.

Traditional Spanish games

Children often find it interesting to play games from another country and culture. Here are a few games which are played by Spanish children:

- **El escondite inglés** – One person stands facing a wall while the others line up at the other end of the playground. The person with their back to the others calls **'uno, dos, tres…'** while the others creep up on them. When the person turns around and shouts: **'sin mover las manos ni los pies'**, which means "without moving your hands or feet", all the others have to be as still as statues. If they are seen moving they have to go back to the beginning. The winner is the one who makes it to the wall without being seen moving.

- **La rayuela** – "Hopscotch" – draw out the hopscotch grid and use it to practise counting in Spanish.

- **Piedra, papel o tijera** – the classic game of "rock, paper, scissors".

Other titles available

Collins Very First Spanish Dictionary and ***Collins Primary Spanish Dictionary*** offer coverage of core vocabulary and have been designed specifically to meet the needs of young learners. Colourfully illustrated and presented in an attractive and easy-to-use layout, both dictionaries encourage learners to build confidence in their language skills.

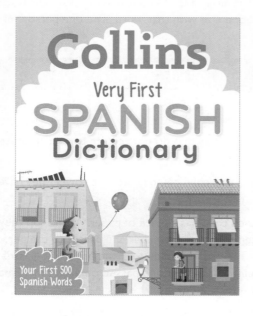

Collins Very First Spanish Dictionary

ISBN	978-0-00-758355-3
Format	272 x 212 mm
Extent	80 pages
Pub Date	19 Jun 2014

Collins Primary Spanish Dictionary
(New Edition in April 2019)

ISBN	978-0-00-831269-5
Format	210 x 148 mm
Extent	640 pages
Pub Date	4 April 2019

E-book version

ISBN	978-0-00-831424-8
Pub Date	4 April 2019